C0-EDW-698

Part
AUG 2 6 1992

Where Animals Live

The World of Eagles

Words by Virginia Harrison
Adapted from Jim Scott's *The Eagle in the Mountains*

Photographs by
Wendy Shattil & Bob Rozinski
Oxford Scientific Films

Gareth Stevens Publishing
Milwaukee

Contents

Where Eagles Live	3	Incubation and Hatching	20
Eagles Around the World	4	Growing Up	22
Eagles in the Mountains	6	Mountain Neighbors	24
The Eagle's Body	8	Eagles and People	26
Flight and Migration	10	The Dangers to Eagles	28
Food and Feeding	12	Life in the Mountains	30
Eagles in Winter	14	Index and New Words	
Courtship and Mating	16	About Eagles	32
Nesting and Laying Eggs	18		

Note: The use of a capital letter for an eagle's name means that it is a *species* of eagle (for example, Bald Eagle). The use of a lowercase, or small, letter means that it is a member of a larger *group* of eagles.

Where Eagles Live

Eagles live in many parts of the world. They are able to fly long distances, with some living in the mountains, some in deserts, some near the ocean, and others in the jungles. Like the American Bald Eagle (above and left), most eagles prefer to live away from people.

Eagles are the largest of the birds of *prey*. They eat most animals smaller than themselves, such as other birds, small mammals, fish, and snakes. They are good *predators* because they can see well and fly fast. Eagles hunt during the day and sleep at night. When food is scarce, they may fly hundreds of miles. Eagles living in the north may *migrate* south in the fall and return in the spring to breed.

Eagles Around the World

Eagles live in many different regions of the world. About 60 *species* of eagles are divided into four main groups: snake eagles, booted eagles, harpy eagles, and sea eagles.

This Black-breasted Snake Eagle eats snakes and other reptiles — as you might expect! All members of the snake eagle family have strong, stubby toes and bright yellow eyes.

The Golden Eagle is in the large family of booted eagles. They are named for the thick covering of feathers on their legs. The Golden Eagle, found in North America, is the most common booted eagle. It flies over mountains, woods, and fields in search of small mammals.

Large and colorful harpy eagles usually live in the jungle, where they may feed on monkeys and other animals.

As a member of the sea eagle family, the American Bald Eagle lives near water and eats fish. It has a wingspan of 6 feet (2 m) or more. The African Fish Eagle (left) looks, acts, and eats like a Bald Eagle. The Bateleur (right), a snake eagle from Africa, prefers mammals to fish.

Eagles in the Mountains

These Bald Eagles perch in the trees surrounding their mountain home.

Eagles live in mountains that vary in size from foothills to the 29,000-foot- (9,000-m-) high Himalayas in Asia. The kinds of mountain *habitats* vary, too. The tops of mountains are a snow-covered, rocky habitat. The *tundra* below the snowcaps is sparsely covered with plants.

Below the tundra is a habitat of forests, streams, or meadows.

Eagles follow their prey with the seasons. In the winter, deer and other large mammals move down the mountainsides. Smaller mammals that live high in the mountains, such as rabbits and squirrels, hibernate. Therefore, eagles must move down in search of food.

Some eagles like to eat water birds and fish. But frozen lakes and streams force water birds to fly south, and fish become unavailable. When spring comes, and the snow and ice melt, the eagles once again search the high mountains for food.

This Golden Eagle hunts in evergreen forests. Tall trees make good vantage points for eagles.

The Eagle's Body

Eagles have sharp beaks for killing prey and tearing flesh apart. They swallow the torn flesh whole and store it in their *crop*, or throat sack.

The size of eagles varies. Their wingspans are shorter if they live where they must fly between trees, and longer if they soar through open air.

Eagles can see eight times farther than humans. A Golden Eagle can see a rabbit 2 miles (3.2 km) away! All eagles have a clear third eyelid to protect their eyes and keep them moist.

During the breeding season, the color of the eagle's *plumage* is very important. It helps the birds identify each other. Once a year eagles gradually lose their feathers and grow new ones. This process is called *molting*.

The sharp claws on an eagle's feet are called *talons*. Eagles use their talons to grasp branches while resting and sleeping as well as for grabbing and killing prey. Each species has a different kind of talon. Fish-eating eagles have *spicules*, or tiny hooks, on their talons for grasping slippery fish. Eagles flex their leg muscles to open and close their talons.

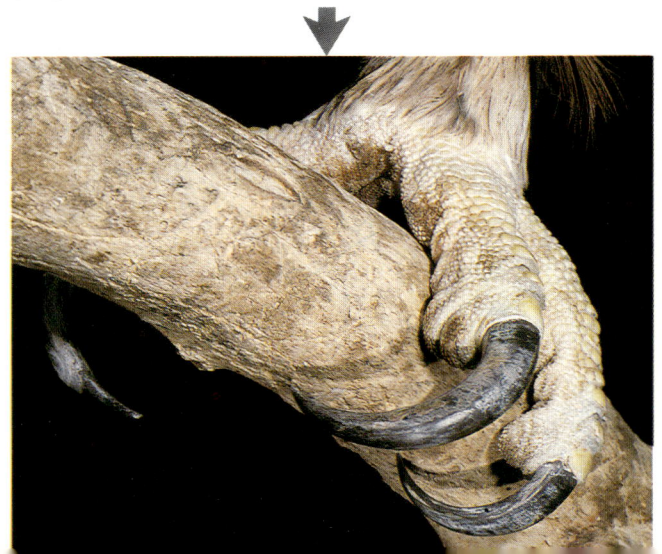

Flight and Migration

Eagles have wings made for soaring and gliding on air currents. As an eagle matures, its feathers change color (upper left). When taking off or flying low, the eagle must flap its wings steadily to remain in the air. Its *wing slots* (upper right) help the bird steer once it is soaring.

Eagles also use their tails to steer. Eagles must travel many miles each day to find food, and their hollow, light bones make the steering and flying easy. When they find *thermals*, or warm air currents, they can soar for long distances without much effort.

With the change of seasons, eagles migrate to different places. In the fall, Bald Eagles may travel hundreds or thousands of miles searching for mild climates and open water, while Golden Eagles may only travel shorter distances.

When migrating, Bald Eagles usually fly when the weather is good and during the warm hours of the afternoon. At night and during rain or snow, eagles will stop and wait. They fly alone but join other eagles at their final stop.

Food and Feeding

Eagles that live near water feed on fish, often sharing their source of food with gulls and other water birds. Bald Eagles fly along rivers and coastlines in search of salmon, diving from high in the air to pull them from the water. They eat the fish on nearby perches. When salmon swim upstream to lay eggs, dozens of eagles gather to feed on these fish.

Bald Eagles may chase other birds, forcing them to drop their fish — often in midair! The eagle then takes the fish to a perch and eats it (below).

Eagles may also eat water birds. An injured or sick duck or goose is easy prey to an eagle. Golden Eagles eat rodents and rabbits. Their strong talons can crush the small bodies of these mammals, and the sharp beaks tear their flesh.

Eagles also eat *carrion*, or dead animal flesh. Bald Eagles may eat dead whales, seals, or other marine mammals washed ashore, while eagles living farther inland may feast on deer carcasses.

An eagle can go for weeks without feeding. If it eats large amounts when food is available, it can live through the times when it is scarce. Undigested fur and bones eventually pass out through the birds' mouths in the form of pellets.

Eagles in Winter

Each fall, Bald Eagles fly south to warmer weather, or east or west to the warmer coastal regions. They arrive in November and stay until March. They gather where food is abundant. In North America, this often means along lakes and rivers, or the Pacific coast of Canada and Alaska.

Bald Eagles may gather in large groups during the winter months. They return to the same areas year after year, and can be seen in groups of hundreds, or even thousands. The Chilkat River in Alaska has the largest group of wintering Bald Eagles in the world. Each fall, they gather in a group of more than 3,000 birds and feed on the breeding salmon. This area is now a refuge, or protected area, for the eagles.

Bald Eagles will share the same roosting areas, and even feed, bathe, and soar together. In the morning, they may fly together in search of food. They may even follow other eagles to common feeding grounds. But for most of the day, they save energy by perching in trees.

Courtship and Mating

Eagles begin mating between the ages of three and six, when they reach full adult plumage. This is a sign the eagle is ready to mate.

In the early spring, the newly mature eagle will select a mate. To make contact with its mate, the eagle often calls from its perch (above). It may stay with this same mate for the rest of its life. This process is called "pair bonding," which is a lot like human marriage.

Once eagles have paired, they warn other eagles to stay away. A pair of breeding eagles will guard their *territory* from other eagles. They may call, perch, or fly around their area as a warning. This protectiveness allows the pair to raise young and hunt for food without much competition or disturbance from other birds.

During courtship, the pair chases through the air, diving and soaring. They may dive toward the ground together, and fly up again at the last second. This is called "roller coastering." Another exciting courtship display is called "cartwheeling." The eagles lock talons while high up, then spiral down toward the ground.

Nesting and Laying Eggs

After eagles mate, they build a huge nest, usually out of large sticks woven together. They may go back to the same nest every year and repair it. Eagles nest on the ground, on ledges, or in trees — as long as they can see their surroundings.

Eagles generally build one nest, but they may maintain two or three in their territory. Biologists believe the extra nests are used if the first one is destroyed. Eagles may also change nests to avoid *parasites*, such as lice. One Golden Eagle pair reportedly had as many as fourteen nests!

The nests take a month to build and are quite heavy. One Bald Eagle's nest weighed almost 2 tons — about the weight of a small car!

Eagles lay between one and four eggs, but usually just two. The group of eggs is called a *clutch*. The brown and white eggs are usually laid two to four days apart.

The nests may be deep or shallow, but they are always lined with soft material such as grass, pine needles, and feathers to give the eggs and the young a soft resting place.

Incubation and Hatching

Eagles hatch about two to three days apart. At first, they cannot even hold up their heads. Gradually, they grow strong and gain weight.

Before the eggs hatch, the adult eagles take turns sitting on the eggs. This is called *incubation*. They sit so their *brood patch* is touching the eggs. This patch is a place on the eagles' breast with few feathers and lots of veins. The warmth of the adults' blood in the veins warms the eggs.

Bald Eagles hatch after 35 days, and Golden Eagles after at least 40 days. This Golden Eagle is still helpless. Its nest is lined with rodent fur.

Just before they hatch, the eaglets cheep inside the eggs. They have a small, sharp "egg tooth" on their beaks which they use to crack open their shells.

When eaglets hatch, they are wet and their eyes are closed. They sleep for the first day while the silky *down* dries off. By the second day, they eat small pieces of meat offered by their parents.

Eaglets weigh only 3 ounces (85 g) when they hatch. If food is scarce the oldest, strongest eaglet may kill the other young to assure its own survival. Golden Eagles will be fed by their parents for several months.

Growing Up

These young Golden Eagles have grown, but they still await their parents' return with food.

When the young finally become able to fly, they are said to *fledge*. Before they can fledge, they must shed the down coat that has covered their bodies for the first three to five weeks, during the "downy stage." After this first coat is shed, a thicker down appears. After a few more weeks, feathers begin to emerge from the down. Once the "feathered stage" is complete, the immature eagle may try to fly.

After eight weeks, the eaglet may have all its feathers, but it still cannot fly. During this time, eaglets *preen* themselves, and the adults return to the nest only to feed their young.

At ten weeks of age, the immature eagles are ready to leave the nest. Their first attempt may be a short or long flight.

After fledging, the young stay near the nest all summer. The parents continue to feed them and teach them how to hunt. This Bald Eagle is on its own, but its white head and tail feathers will take several years to develop.

Mountain Neighbors

Eagles share the mountains with many other animals. Some, like this Black Bear (left), may compete with eagles for food. Others, like this Cottontail Rabbit (right), must be wary of becoming prey for eagles and other predators.

Trout and salmon are some of the many species of fish found in the mountain lakes and streams. Beavers and muskrats are water mammals that live and eat in the lakes and streams.

Many kinds of deer, such as these young Mule Deer, are common in the meadows of the mountain habitat.

Hawks and falcons are smaller meat-eating birds that share the mountain habitat with the eagle. They also have keen eyesight and strong wings that help them catch their prey. This Northern Harrier (above) flies low in search of prey. It has caught an unlucky duck.

Smaller birds such as songbirds, crows, Blue Jays, and swallows live in the mountains. Mountain bats hang upside-down in caves, leaving at night to eat insects.

Eagles and People

Long the subject of art, songs, legends, and even stories in the Bible, the eagle has stood for power, courage, and immortality. Some Indians in the northwestern United States and Canada still carve the eagle's image into their wooden totem poles (below). A member of the Tlingit tribe of Alaska wove this beaded apron (right).

In 1782, the Bald Eagle was adopted as the national emblem of the United States. Its picture can be found on US coins and bills and on the official seal of the United States. Several other countries also use the eagle as their emblem.

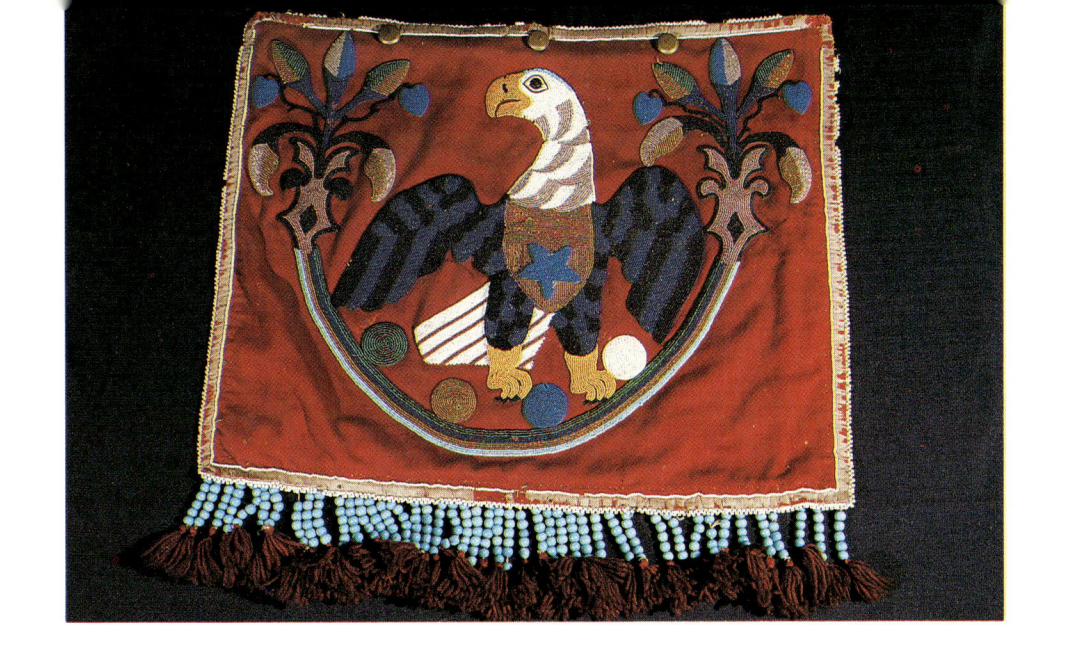

But despite our admiration for the eagle, it has suffered from human maltreatment. Sadly, at least twenty species of eagle are listed as *endangered*, or in danger of disappearing forever. The Bald Eagle is one such species. Concerned people are helping to keep eagles healthy and safe.

The Dangers to Eagles

Eagles are more threatened by people than by other wildlife. Eagles have few natural enemies because they are predators, but humans have killed eagles and spoiled their habitat for years.

While humans continue to destroy natural habitats by building roads and towns, eagles are losing their territories. Along with human development of the land comes the poisoning of the water and the air. Fish take in the poisons, and so, too, do the eagles that eat them.

Many people are trying to help the eagles now. People work at places that nurse sick and injured eagles back to health. When the eagles recover, they are released back into the wild.

Over the years, people have shot eagles that were, for the most part, unjustly blamed for killing farm animals. In Great Britain, the European Sea Eagle was killed off completely in the early 1900s because farmers thought it was killing their lambs. In the US, many Bald and Golden Eagles have been killed over the past two hundred years for the same reason.

Today, it is illegal to hurt eagles or destroy their nests and eggs. The *pesticide* DDT has been outlawed in some countries, and many deadly power lines now have protective coatings to protect eagles and other birds.

Life in the Mountains

As predators, eagles are at the top of their food chain. Through food chains, energy from the sun and *nutrients* from the soil flow from the plants that animals eat to the animals that eat those animals, and so on. When all these living things die, their bodies *decompose*, and the nutrients are returned to the earth.

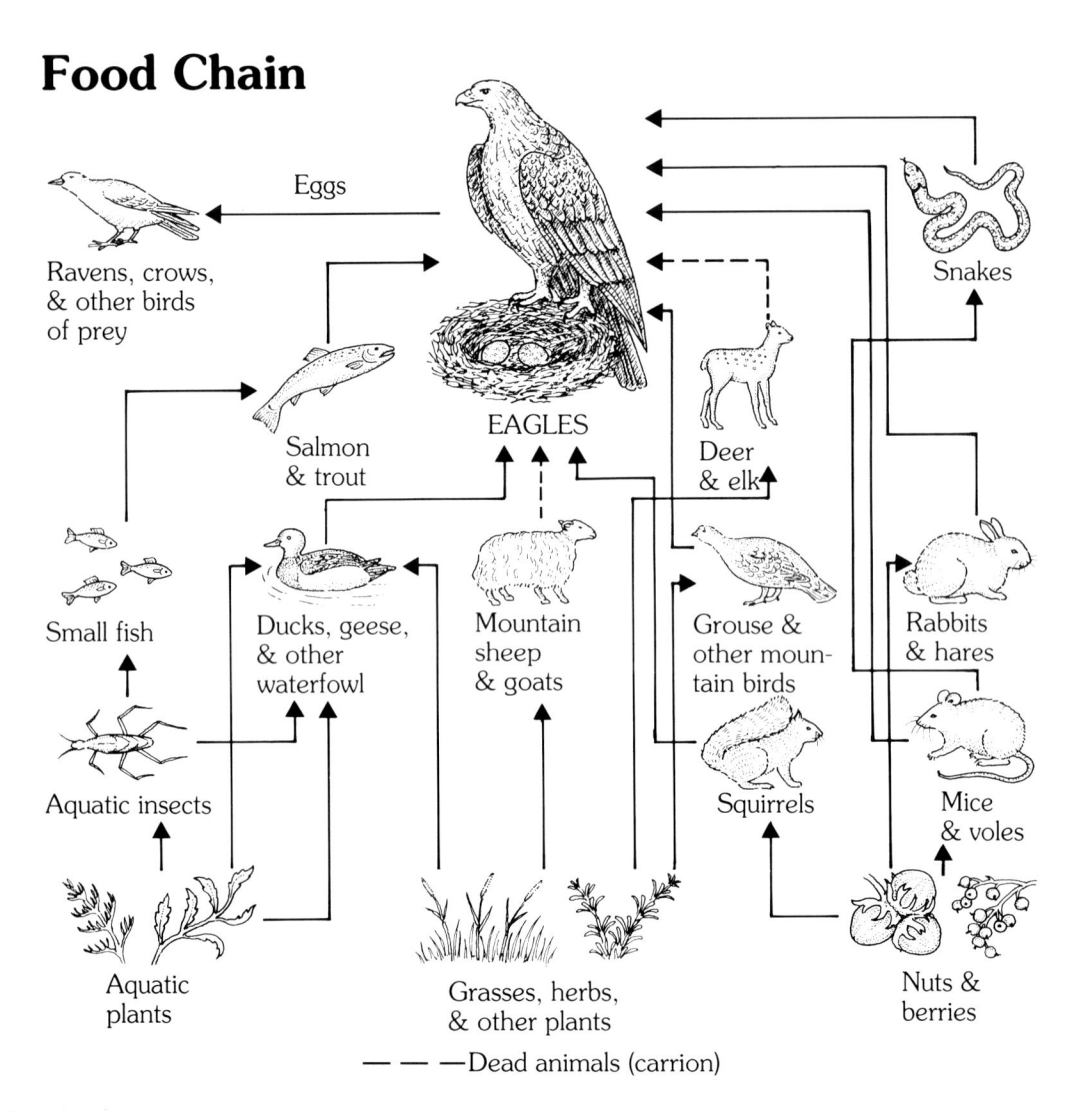

Food Chain

Ravens, crows, & other birds of prey

Eggs

EAGLES

Snakes

Salmon & trout

Deer & elk

Small fish

Ducks, geese, & other waterfowl

Mountain sheep & goats

Grouse & other mountain birds

Rabbits & hares

Aquatic insects

Squirrels

Mice & voles

Aquatic plants

Grasses, herbs, & other plants

Nuts & berries

— — —Dead animals (carrion)

⬆

All life is connected by the food chain, including the majestic eagle. Today, people are starting to understand how important food chains are to life on our planet. So in order to protect our *environment*, we must protect both the animals and their habitat.

We must respect the eagle and all other living things that share the planet Earth.

Index and New Words About Eagles

These new words about eagles appear in the text on the pages shown after each definition. Each new word first appears in the text in *italics*, just as it appears here.

brood patch .. bare area of skin on breasts of adult birds, used to keep eggs warm. **20**

carrion .... the dead flesh of animals. **13, 30**

clutch .... a set of eggs. **19**

crop .... a pouch in a bird's gullet for storing food. **8**

down .... the first covering of soft feathers on a chick's body. **21, 22**

endangered .. threatened with extinction. **27**

environment . the surroundings in which plants and animals live. **31**

fledge .... to take the first flight. **22, 23**

habitat .... the natural home of plants or animals. **6, 7, 24, 25, 28, 31**

incubation .... keeping eggs warm so they will hatch. **20**

migrate .... for animals, to move seasonally from one region or climate to another. **3, 11**

molting .... shedding and replacing feathers with new ones. **9**

nutrients ...... vitamins and other substances in food that animals and plants need to grow. **30**

parasite .... an organism that lives and feeds on another organism. **18**

pesticides ..... poisonous chemicals sprayed on crops to protect them from harmful insects. **29**

plumage .... the feathers covering a bird's body. **9, 16**

predator .... an animal that kills and eats other animals. **3, 24**

preen .... to clean and oil feathers with the bill. **23**

prey .... an animal that is killed by another for food. **3, 7, 8, 9, 13, 24, 25, 30**

species .... a particular kind of animal or plant. **2, 4, 9, 24, 27**

spicules .... sharp spikes on the toes of fish eagles. **9**

talons .... the claws of birds of prey. **9, 13, 17**

territory .... area of land which an animal defends against intruders. **17, 18, 28**

thermals .... rising currents of warm air in the atmosphere. **10**

tundra .... cold, treeless area above the timberline. **6, 7**

wing slots ..... gaps between feathers on the tips of eagles' wings. **10**

Reading level analysis: SPACHE 2.7, FRY 3, FLESCH 90 (very easy), FOG 5, SMOG 3

Library of Congress Cataloging-in-Publication Data

Harrison, Virginia, 1966-
    The world of eagles / words by Virginia Harrison ; adapted from Jim Scott's The eagle in the mountains ; photographs by Wendy Shattil & Bob Rozinski of Oxford Scientific Films.
                  p. cm -- (Where animals live)
      Summary: Photographs and text depict eagles in their natural habitats, illustrating how they feed, defend themselves, and breed.
      ISBN 0-8368-0138-5
    1. Eagles--Juvenile literature. [1. Eagles.] I. Shattil, Wendy, ill. II. Rozinski, Robert, ill. III. Scott, James A., 1946- Eagle in the mountains. IV. Oxford Scientific Films. V. Title. VI. Series.
    QL696.F32H37   1989
    598'.916--dc20   89-4459

North American edition first published in 1989 by Gareth Stevens, Inc., 7317 West Green Tree Road, Milwaukee, WI 53223, USA US edition, this format, copyright © 1989 by Belitha Press Ltd. Text copyright © 1989 by Gareth Stevens, Inc. All rights reserved. No part of this book may be reproduced in any form or by any means without permission in writing from Gareth Stevens, Inc. First conceived, designed, and produced by Belitha Press Ltd., London, as **The Eagle in the Mountains**, with an original text copyright by Oxford Scientific Films. Format copyright by Belitha Press Ltd.
Series Editor: Mark J. Sachner. Art Director: Treld Bicknell. Design: Naomi Games. Cover Design: Gary Moseley. Line Drawings: Lorna Turpin.

The author and publishers wish to thank the following for permission to reproduce copyright material: **Wendy Shattil and Robert Rozinski** for pp. 1, 2, 3, 6, 7, 8 both, 9 both, 10 both, 11 both, 12 both, 13, 14, 15, 16 both, 17, 20 both, 21, 22 both, 23, 24 both, 25 both, 26, 27 below, 28 both, 29, 31, back cover; Oxford Scientific Films Ltd. for front cover (Animals Animals — Lynn M. Stone), pp. 4 above (Animals Animals — Stouffer Enterprises Inc.), 4 below (Roy Coombes), 5 both (Stan Osolinski), 18 (Animals Animals — Philip Hart), 19 above (Animals Animals — Charles Palek), 19 below (Animals Animals — Harold E. Wilson); p. 27 above is courtesy of the Denver Museum of Natural History, Denver, Colorado.

Printed in the United States of America
1 2 3 4 5 6 7 8 9 95 94 93 92 91 90 89
For a free color catalog describing Gareth Stevens' list of high-quality children's books call 1 (800) 433-0942

The world of eagles /
J 598.916 H   31814850077931
Harrison, Virginia,   1st Americ
    PORTAGE PUBLIC LIB   10110

J598.916   AUG 2 6 1992   Por.
  H
        Harrison, Virginia
           The world of eagles

                Portage Public Library